BIBLE
Comes to Life

Book 2
THE FALL

Joy Sukadi | Lilyana Margaretha

BIBLE COMES TO LIFE

BOOK 2: THE FALL

© 2023 by Joy Sukadi and Lilyana Margaretha

All rights reserved. No part of this book may be reproduced in any form without permission in writing from the publisher, except in the case of brief quotations embodied in critical articles or reviews.

Unless otherwise indicated, all Scripture quotations are taken from the Holy Bible, New Living Translation, copyright © 1996, 2004, 2015 by Tyndale House Foundation. Used by permission of Tyndale House Publishers, Inc., Carol Stream, Illinois 60188. All rights reserved.

Scripture quotations marked NIV are taken from the Holy Bible, New International Version®, NIV®. Copyright © 1973, 1978, 1984, 2011 by Biblica, Inc.® Used by permission. All rights reserved worldwide.

Scripture quotations marked MSG are taken from the Holy Bible, The Message. Copyright © 1993, 2002, 2018 by Eugene H. Peterson.

Scripture quotations marked NIrV are taken from the Holy Bible, New International Reader's Version®, NIrV®. Copyright © 1995, 1996, 1998, 2014 by Biblica, Inc.® Used by permission of Zondervan. All rights reserved worldwide. www.zondervan.com. The "NIrV" and "New International Reader's Version" are trademarks registered in the United States Patent and Trademark Office by Biblica, INC.™

All emphasis in Scripture has been added.

Editor: Pam Lagomarsino

Interior and Cover Design: Rachdian Topasca

Cover Image: Kreker Kate and Febri Kurniawan

A list of photo/image credits is at the end of this book.

ISBN: 978-1-7376802-1-5

Published by Sharpening Little Arrows, LLC
Mill Creek, WA 98012
www.sharpeninglittlearrows.com
E-mail: sharpeninglittlearrows@gmail.com

Welcome to Bible Comes to Life!..........................5

Introduction..10

Quick Start Guide..11

Material List...12

2-1: True or False?.......................................15

2-2: Temptations: "Just One Bite!".....................35

2-3: The Invisible Enemy................................49

2-4: Unbreakable...61

2-5: A Fallen World......................................75

2-6: A Clean Heart.......................................89

Truth Blast!... 102

Notes.. 106

Photo Credits.. 107

About The Authors.................................... 108

Welcome to Bible Comes to Life!

"Equipping Children with Biblical Truths to Challenge Cultural Lies"

DEAR FRIENDS,

Our journey started in 2019 as our children were elementary school age. We observed the world around us and noticed we are raising our children in a different day and age now. They are bombarded daily with progressive agendas, lies, perversity, and non-biblical views through social media, TV shows, books, and many more. This simple question filled our hearts: how do we equip our children to stand strong against popular beliefs and cultural lies? The current is strong; the pressure is great. We heard so many stories of kids with Christian upbringing turn away from their faith once they go to college (or even earlier!).

During that discouraging time, God spoke clearly in our hearts: **"Daughters, you cannot stop the flood from coming, but you can start building an ark for your family—intentionally and with a purpose. Your family will be saved!"** We could not stop the non-biblical culture from bombarding our children, but we could win this battle by equipping them from the inside out! In this saturated "woke" culture, sending our children to Sunday schools, youth groups, or summer Bible camps will not be enough anymore. Discipleship and equipping need to happen every day, in our homes, by the closest people raising them—*us!* The Word of God in Psalm 127:4 (NIV) resonated loud and clear in our hearts:

> *"Like arrows in the hands of a warrior are children born in one's youth."*

As parents, we are called to shape our next generation so they can be as sharp as arrows. We are assigned to raise sons and daughters of clarity who can detect the enemy's lies from hundreds of miles away. We must equip them daily with biblical truths so they can push back the darkness and defend the truth. The Bible tells us in 1 Peter 3:15:

> "Instead, you must worship Christ as Lord of your life. And if someone asks about your hope as a believer, always be ready to explain it."

In creating this "Bible Comes to Life" series, we pray that you will find resources to do intentional discipleship in the heart of your homes. This series will help you instill biblical values into your children's hearts in relevant and engaging ways. The best part of all: we use science, apologetics, and logical explanations to support these biblical truths. We know children are highly visual beings with short attention spans. Their curious minds respond best to exciting games, science experiments, arts and crafts, and compelling story-telling from their parents. Even Jesus talks in parables.

With constant streams of games and entertainment surrounding our children, the Bible could become an archaic and irrelevant resource for them. Our vision is to bring the Bible to life again by presenting God's Word in the most exciting, creative ways. We want kids to experience, taste, and see how real and magnificent our Creator is.

We designed this book series for busy families like yours and mine. In each lesson, we compare a non-biblical worldview and a biblical worldview. We then support the biblical values with hands-on activities, science experiments, arts and crafts, or games to make the Bible relevant. These activities are optional, but they can promote fun family time on the weekends, during summer break, or even during the busiest weeknights.

Finally, at the end of each lesson, you will find intriguing questions to foster a meaningful family discussion. This time provides opportunities for us parents, to open up about your past, tell heartfelt stories, and "download" unforgettable truths into your children's hearts. This book basically kills two birds with one stone: creating a strong bond within your family while also building a solid biblical foundation in your children's lives. See this book as your eternal investment to launch your children into the world ready to defend their Christian faith. We are excited to be on this journey with you!

For our children's souls,
Joy and Lilyana

Book 2

The Fall

For everyone has sinned;
we all fall short of God's glorious standard.
Romans 3:23

Introduction

As parents, we would always cherish those newborn moments: the seemingly perfect bundle of joy, tiny fingers and toes, and heartwarming smiles that brighten our sleepless nights. Then, the first mistake happened: the first fall, the first fight with siblings, the first act of disobedience, or the first stinky attitude. Those challenging moments are bound to come our way. The truth is:

Every human heart is sinful in nature, even from the beginning of time.

Do you remember the first-ever human mistake? It was not the mistake of the Creator, but it was the sin of His *creation*. Creating humans came with its own set of risks. Disobedience was at the top of the list. It's a risk God was fully aware of and willing to take because of His love for us.

The devil might have laughed in victory when the first humans took a bite of the forbidden fruit. Little did he know, God would declare right away His beautiful promise of a Savior who will crush the enemy's head. God is not blindsided by the human fall. The Creator never made a mistake. It's a risk well thought out even before human creation.

Navigating this dark and fallen world will not be easy. As a result of sin, we see war, pandemics, natural disasters, and racial injustices all around us. However, one thing is for sure: God, the **Promise-Maker**, is still in control—even until today. He is sovereign, and His love never fails. His promise stays true for His children: "For I am the Lord your God who takes hold of your right hand and says to you, Do not fear; I will help you" (Isaiah 41:13 NIV).

Through the lessons in this book, we will learn about **God's unfailing love**. He could have destroyed or abandoned His fallen creations. But instead, He "clothed them" with love and compassion to cover their shame and nakedness. As we recognize patterns of sin, temptations, and failures, we will encounter the God of second chances. He is strong and holy—yet faithful and full of compassion. Let's begin!

Quick Start Guide

We know you are eager to jump into the lessons. But before you do, here are a few important things to note.

Each chapter contains a lesson ready to be read aloud by the parent(s). In each lesson, you will find:

- Purpose
- Icebreaker (either questions, a mini-game, or a short story)
- Introduction
- Non-biblical View
- Biblical View
- Activity (including materials and instructions): science experiments, engineering, games, arts and crafts, or cooking.
- Discussion
- Summary
- Truth to Remember
- Memory Verse
- Fact Check (in some lessons)

The instructions in the **Activity** sections are a guideline for parents. Although you will find most materials easily in your house, we recommend checking the Activity section at least a few days before the lesson to prepare the materials.

The **Discussion** section has expected answers in parentheses for questions that need definite answers. Some questions also have additional read-aloud parts to solidify the truths and make connections after children give their answers.

At the end of some lessons is a **Fact Check** section for parents and older children to dig deeper into the Scripture, scientific and historical facts, or other resources.

At the end of this book, you will find the **"Truth Blast!"** section. Here, we compiled a list of Truths and key Bible verses from all the lessons. Check out this section as you go along the lessons to see how each lesson ties into the big picture and for a quick reference in the future.

Last but not least, find extra resources (links to videos and articles) at our website: **www.sharpeninglittlearrows.com**

Material List

As promised, we want to make it as easy as possible for you to use this book. So, we put together a list of all materials you will need in the lessons for your quick reference.

2-1 WATER OPTICAL ILLUSION

Note: There are two simple experiments for this lesson. You may choose to do either one or both.

- Paper (about 2 x 2 inches)
- A pen or marker
- A clear drinking glass or jar
- Water
- A ruler
- A drinking straw

2-2 THE BALLOON VS. THE BOTTLE

- A glass bottle or medium-sized jar
- Balloons
- A few strips of paper (about 3 x 1 inches) or post-it notes (folded to make paper strips)
- Lighter or matches
- A drinking straw

2-3 EAGLE VS. CHICKEN GAME

- A blanket or any silly props (optional)

2-4 RAINBOW SPAGHETTI

Note: This activity involves cooking and enjoying a meal together. Plan ahead to determine when you want to start the lesson.

- A large cooking pot
- One pound of uncooked spaghetti
- Four to six tablespoons melted butter (or olive oil)
- Food coloring (various colors—at least one per family member)
- Sealable plastic sandwich bags (as many as the number of colors used)
- Colander
- Freshly grated parmesan cheese
- Salt and pepper
- Water

2-5 SCRATCH ART

- White paper (Thicker materials will work better.)
- Wax crayons or oil pastels
- Black crayon or acrylic paint
- Toothpick (or other pointy objects, such as skewers, chopsticks, screwdriver, or paperclip)
- Paintbrush (optional)
- Picture frames (optional)

2-6 SIN JARS

- Clear jars or drinking glasses—one for each family member
- Food coloring
- Condiments, such as soy sauce, fish sauce, tomato ketchup, or vinegar (optional)
- Water

2-1

True or False?

2-1 True or False

PURPOSE

To learn what our standard of truth is and not rely on human perceptions and popular opinions.

Icebreaker

- Let's play **"Simon Says."** Do the actions only when I start with "Simon says."

  Note to parents:
  - Try inserting some tricks, such as saying, "Simon says: touch your ears" while you touch your nose.
  - After several tricks, say these two sentences as the final tricks:
    1. "Simon says: say 'I love you.'"
    2. "Simon says: say 'I love you four times.'"

- Which one is right: *"I love you, I love you, I love you, I love you"* or *"I love you four times"*? That's tricky, right?

Similar to our tricky game, our world is full of mixed-up truth and confusion. This began a long time ago, shortly after God created Adam and Eve. Let's take a closer look at their story (Genesis 3:1–4).

The devil, looking like a snake, tricked Eve by asking, "Did God really say you must not eat the fruit from *any of the trees* in the garden?" He was very sneaky!

Eve then said, "Of course we may eat fruit from the trees in the garden…It's only the fruit from the tree in the middle of the garden that we are not allowed to eat. God said, 'You must not eat it or even touch it; if you do, you will die.'"

Hold on, did God say not to touch it? No! God only said not to *eat* it. The devil's trick was to confuse Eve, and it's working! She **began to doubt if what God said was real.**

And then the snake said, "You won't die!" But, is it really true they won't die? (**Hint**: Check what God said in Genesis 2:16–17. He warned them not to eat it, or else they *will* die.)

The story continued. Adam and Eve believed the devil's lies and did the first sin. The devil *twisted* God's command to make them turn away from the truth. The devil is the ultimate liar!

. . .

NON-BIBLICAL VIEW

The bad news is the devil is still working today. He tries to turn us away from the truth and plays tricks with our minds into believing his lies. He often covers up his lies, so they seem to be right and even good for us.

How can we know what's true, partly true, or completely false?

Who should we ask to get the right answers: our parents? our friends? Google?

BIBLICAL VIEW

The good news is God gave us the answers in the Bible! In **2 Timothy 3:16**, Paul said,

> *"All Scripture is inspired by God and is useful to teach us what is true and to make us realize what is wrong in our lives. It corrects us when we are wrong and teaches us to do what is right."*

The Bible tells us the real, honest truth— not just what we think is true or what the enemy says is true.

2-1 True or False

Did you know?

- ☑ **Fact #1: Around forty people wrote the Bible over 1,500 years.**
  They came from various backgrounds and times, such as an Egyptian noble (Moses), a shepherd (David), a Babylonian official (Daniel), a tax collector (Matthew), a doctor (Luke), a fisherman (Peter), a rabbi (Paul), and more. Yet, they all talked about the *same* Messiah with the same accurate details.

- ☑ **Fact #2: The Bible has 66 books: 39 in the Old Testament and 27 in the New Testament.**
  These books tell a big story about God, including creation, how humans started sinning, and how God sent Jesus to save us for our sins.

- ☑ **Fact #3: The Bible is the *bestselling* book in the world and in history.**
  It has been translated into 1,200 languages.

- ☑ **Fact #4: The Bible was the first book ever printed in Europe in 1454.**[1]

. . .

Have you seen a shiny spot of water on a hot road on a sunny day? When you get closer, you realize there's nothing there. This happens a lot in the desert. Imagine feeling so thirsty and then finding out it's just a trick. It's not fun at all! This is called a **mirage**, and it is an **optical illusion** that tricks our brains.

Today, we will explore how our brains work and "see" things. Interestingly, our brains can sometimes guess wrongly and tell us what they think is right, just like how a mirage works.

Activity

Water Optical Illusion

MATERIALS
- Paper (about 2 x 2 inches)
- A pen or marker
- A clear drinking glass or jar
- Water
- A ruler
- A drinking straw

Note: Two different experiments are available here. You may choose to do either one or both.

2-1 True or False

INSTRUCTIONS

EXPERIMENT #1

1. Draw an arrow on a piece of paper and write the word "RIGHT" below it.

2. Fill a clear glass with water and put it on the table.
3. Place the paper right behind the glass of water, touching the glass wall.

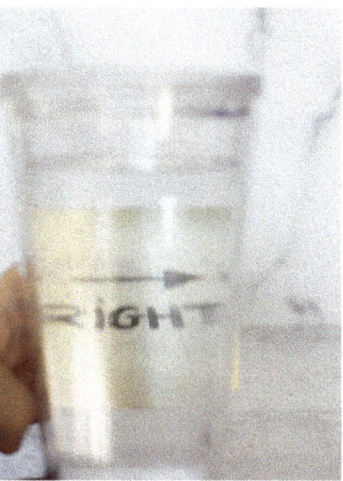

4. Check the drawing on the paper while looking through the water. Make sure the paper and your eyes are at the same level.

5. Observe how the arrow and the word "RIGHT" look.

6. Put a ruler next to the glass.

   Note: The ruler helps to measure the distance as you move the paper away from the glass in the next steps.

7. Slowly move the paper further away from the glass. Stop at about two inches behind the glass.

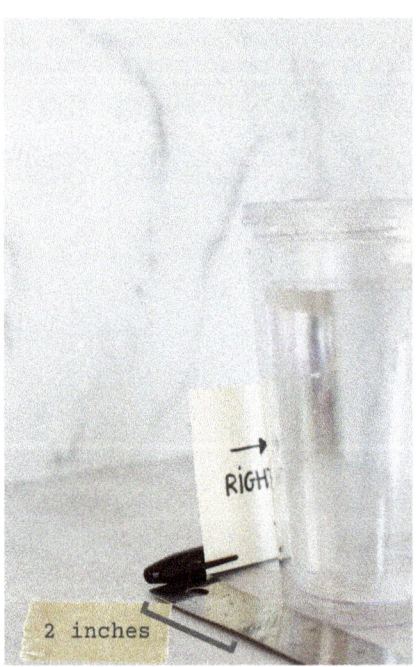 

8. Observe the arrow's direction and the word "RIGHT" while the paper is moving and at two inches away.

9. Continue moving the paper away from the glass. Stop at about four inches behind the glass.

10. Observe the arrow's direction and the word "RIGHT" while the paper is moving and finally at four inches away.

11. If there is extra time, repeat the experiment with other things drawn or written on the paper.

EXPERIMENT #2

1. Hold a straw upright in a glass of water. Bend down so your eyes are level with the water surface.

   Look at how the straw appears.

2. Gently tilt the straw and watch how it looks on the water surface. Ask:

   "How does the straw look when tilted?"

3. Raise the glass of water with the straw inside. Check out the straw from below the water surface. Ask:

   "How does the straw look now?"

2-1 True or False

1. In the first experiment, what happened when we moved the paper away from the glass of water?

   (**Answer:** *As we looked through the glass of water, the drawing/text became blurry and seemed to merge at two inches away. When we moved it farther, the drawing/text completely flipped from what was on the paper.)*

2. In the second experiment, when we looked at the straw from different angles, how did it look? Was it what truly happened to the straw?

   (**Answer:** *The straw might look "broken" or "bent" or even changed in size. But if we pull the straw out of the water, we will know the truth: The straw does not change.)*

2-1 True or False

3. Today's experiments show us "optical illusions," which happen when light bends as it passes through different things like air and water. In these experiments, our eyes "trick" our brains as we see objects through different things. It seems like our brains see things wrongly!

   How do we make sure what we see is really true?

   _____
   _____
   _____
   _____

   (**Answer:** *By checking on the real object without looking through a glass of water or other things.*)

   For more explanation and examples of optical illusions, check out this resource: theconversation.com/curious-kids-how-does-an-optical-illusion-work-123008. [2]

4. In life, what can we use as a guide to show us what is always true? (**Hint:** Read 2 Timothy 3:16 and Joshua 1:8.)

   _____
   _____
   _____
   _____

   (**Answer:** *The Bible is always true and would be the perfect guide for us.*)

   God has made His Word come alive in the Bible. Everything in it is true and teaches us to do what's right. Joshua 1:8 shares God's recipe for success: **study** and **think about His Word**. When we know the Bible well, we can use it as our guide to know what's right and wrong, as it holds the real truth.

   We should not trust only what people say. Our friends, the Internet, and teachers might not always give us the right information. Their "truth" could be influenced by their own thoughts, experiences, and beliefs that might not even be true.

5. Have you ever come across a truth that's been changed or only partially true? For example: "It's okay to do a sin during the week as long as you go to church on Sundays to ask God to forgive you." Is this true?

_____
_____
_____

Play "True or False" game with the children. Let them answer after each sentence. You can choose some examples from the next pages or do all of them.

2-1 True or False

Statement	True or False?
	Answer
Jesus is God.	
	(**Answer:** True. Jesus was not just a good man or prophet. See John 10:30 and Hebrews 1:8.)
Jesus sinned.	
	(**Answer:** False. Jesus was tempted but did not sin. See Hebrews 4:15.)
Jesus is one of many ways to heaven.	
	(**Answer:** False. This might sound tricky, especially for children exposed to the idea of "co-exist" or pluralism in public schools or from the media. Jesus is the only way to heaven. See John 14:6.)
The Bible is a human book. Some stories might have been made up.	
	(**Answer:** False. The Bible says God breathed life into <u>all</u> Scripture, not just some of them. See 2 Timothy 3:16 and the Fact Check section about why the Bible is reliable.)
The Bible is the Word of God and has the real truth.	
	(**Answer:** True. The Bible teaches us what is true and to do what is right. See 2 Timothy 3:16-17.)

True or False?

Statement	Answer
God wouldn't punish sinners. He is love.	*(**Answer:** False. The Bible says the wages of sin is death. Our sins separated us from God. See Romans 6:23 and Isaiah 59:2.)*
We should not tell others they are wrong if they believe they are right. It's not our role to discuss their mistakes. Our role is to show love, accepting them for who they are, regardless of their choices.	*(**Answer:** False. Only God decides what is right and wrong. In fact, we are living in a time similar to Judges 17:6 when people did anything they thought was right. The Bible reminds us to speak the truth in love. See Ephesians 4:15.)*

Note to parents:
You can discuss topics like purity and sex before marriage, abortion, or gender identity issues as examples for older children.

Summary

We shouldn't trust just human opinions or our feelings to know what's true or false. If we are not careful, we might believe whatever the world claims are true and right. Don't let our thoughts and feelings guide our actions, as they might not be true. Instead, use **God's Word** as the **reliable guide**.

2-1 True or False

Truth to Remember

God alone is the source of truth.

God's Word in the Bible tells us the real truth.

Study this Book of Instruction continually.
Meditate on it day and night
so you will be sure to obey everything written in it.
Only then will you prosper and succeed in all you do.

Joshua 1:8

2-1 True or False

2-1 True or False

FACT CHECK

IS THE BIBLE RELIABLE?

Dr. Ken Boa and Mr. Sid Litke talked about different evidence showing the Bible is trustworthy.[3,4] Here's a quick summary for your reference:

1. **Historical records**: Other history books or writings also talked about the same people, places, and events that we read about in the Bible. For example, in his books *Antiquities of the Jews*, the first-century Jewish historian Flavius Josephus mentioned John the Baptist, Jesus, and James by name. Josephus also gave many background details found in the four Gospels and the book of Acts.

2. **Archeological findings**: Many artifacts (old objects) support the Bible. For instance, tablets from 1500 BC were discovered before World War II. They provide useful details that match the stories in Genesis. *(See the details about these tablets on Dr. Ken Boa's website.)*

3. **Fulfilled prophecies**: The Bible has many prophecies (predictions) that came true. For example, Jesus fulfilled over 300 prophecies about the Savior mentioned in the Old Testament. There are more examples of fulfilled prophecies listed in the table below.

Prophecies	Actual History
"THE DESTRUCTION OF THE CITY OF TYRE" • Predicted by Ezekiel (Ezekiel 26:3-4) • Written about 600 BC	• Around 1000 BC, Tyre (now in Lebanon) was rich and had a trade deal with King David of Israel. The king of Tyre gave cedar trees from Lebanon to King Solomon to build the temple and the king's palace. • In 332 BC, Alexander the Great completely destroyed the city of Tyre.

Prophecies	Actual History
"FOUR POWERFUL KINGDOMS WOULD COME ONE AFTER THE OTHER" • Predicted by Daniel (Daniel 2 & 7) • Written about 535 BC	• In the following centuries, four empires (**Babylon, Persia, Greece, and Rome**) rose and fell just like what Daniel had prophesied. • Babylon rose around the 7th and 6th centuries BC but fell to Persians in 539 BC. • Persians were defeated by Alexander the Great of Greece in 331 BC. • Lastly, Rome conquered Greece in 146 BC.

4. **Internal evidence:** Forty writers of the Bible wrote stories and predictions in various times and places, even hundreds of years apart. Yet, their stories match and agree with each other.

Bible Comes to Life: Book 3 Redemption will present more evidence (both historical and archaeological findings) about Jesus, His fulfilled prophecies, the cross, and the resurrection.

WHAT DOES IT MEAN BY "THE BIBLE WAS BREATHED OUT BY GOD"?

It means God directs the human authors of the Bible to record exactly what God wanted and planned, using their own writing styles and personalities. God did not dictate the Bible word by word to them, but He guided and inspired them in their writings.

These writings were later collected to form the Bible as we know it today. Ultimately, the Bible was authored by God, even though humans played a role in writing it.

2-2
Temptations: "Just One Bite!"

2-2 Temptations: "Just One Bite!"

PURPOSE

To teach our children that the enemy will always find ways to tempt them to sin, but God will always provide a way out.

Icebreaker

- Have you ever tried fishing before? Or, have you ever seen anyone fish in cartoons or movies?

- People often use **bait** for fishing. Do you know what bait is for?
  (*Answer:* to attract the fish and hide the hook at the end of the fishing line)

- What do people usually use as bait?
  (*Answer:* worms, insects, leeches, etc.)

2-2 Temptations: "Just One Bite!"

What do you remember about the story of Adam and Eve from the first chapter? At first, they lived happily with God in the Garden of Eden. Imagine them riding on the elephants, playing with the lions, and enjoying yummy snacks whenever they wanted to. Sounds like so much fun, right?

One day, the serpent came and tempted them to eat the fruit from the Tree of Knowledge of Good and Evil. "Just one bite, you won't die," whispered the creature.

When Eve took a bite, she didn't stop there. She asked Adam to eat the fruit too. They both fell into temptation and **did the first-ever sin in the world!**

. . .

Today, we will talk about temptation and how it works. **Temptation** occurs when we desire to do something we know we shouldn't, like wanting a cookie before dinner or secretly watching a TV show our parents say is not good for us.

Temptation works like bait. It lures people in and encourages them to take a bite. "Just one bite, it's okay," temptation whispers in a convincing voice. But behind the temptation is a "hook" that can trap people and cause them to sin again and again! *(To learn more about sin, see the Fact Check section.)*

It always starts with "just one bite," doesn't it?

One nibble of that cupcake.

One sip of the sugary soda.

One tap to begin the video game.

One glance at the magazine or movie.

One lie to skip a class.

One choice to cheat on a test.

Imagine holding a bag of your favorite but not-so-healthy snack. *(Name some snacks your kids like.)* We might say: *I'll have just one bite*. But usually, that one bite could make us eat a whole bag of unhealthy food!

2-2 Temptations: "Just One Bite!"

NON-BIBLICAL VIEW

The world will tell us it's okay to take "one bite" as long as our parents don't find out, as long as it makes us feel good, or as long as we ace our test. They will tempt us with words like:

"Everyone else is doing it too."

"Just trying it once won't hurt!"

"No one will ever know."

"Don't be such a wimp!"

"It's just five more minutes on the video game. It's not a big deal!"

"Nobody likes that kid at school, so it's okay for me to be mean too."

Which ones have you heard before?

Temptation makes us think:

This is *my* life. I have the right to choose whatever I want to do.

2-2 Temptations: "Just One Bite!"

BIBLICAL VIEW

The Bible says we should not play around with temptations. Don't get anywhere near them, think about trying, and even take "just one bite." We should quickly get away from them (2 Timothy 2:22). Move fast! Run away! Leave immediately!

> Sin is like a snowball.
> It gets bigger when we don't stop.

And do you know the result of sin? Yes, it's death—being apart from God and all the good things He planned for us, forever. **Romans 6:23** tells us, "For the wages of sin is death."

When we give in to a temptation, it can make us repeat the same sin over and over again. If it turns into a habit, it's tough to escape from. But here's the good news: God will always show us a way out.

Our activity today will help us be "the smartest fish in the pond." When we see a shiny worm on a hook, let's **swim away from it, not towards it!**

2-2 Temptations: "Just One Bite!"

Activity

The Balloon Vs. The Bottle

MATERIALS

- A glass bottle or medium-sized jar
- Balloons
- A few strips of paper (about 3 x 1 inches) or post-it notes (folded to make paper strips)
- Lighter or matches
- A drinking straw

Note: If you are using a jar, change the word "bottle" with "jar" wherever you see it in the instructions and discussion.

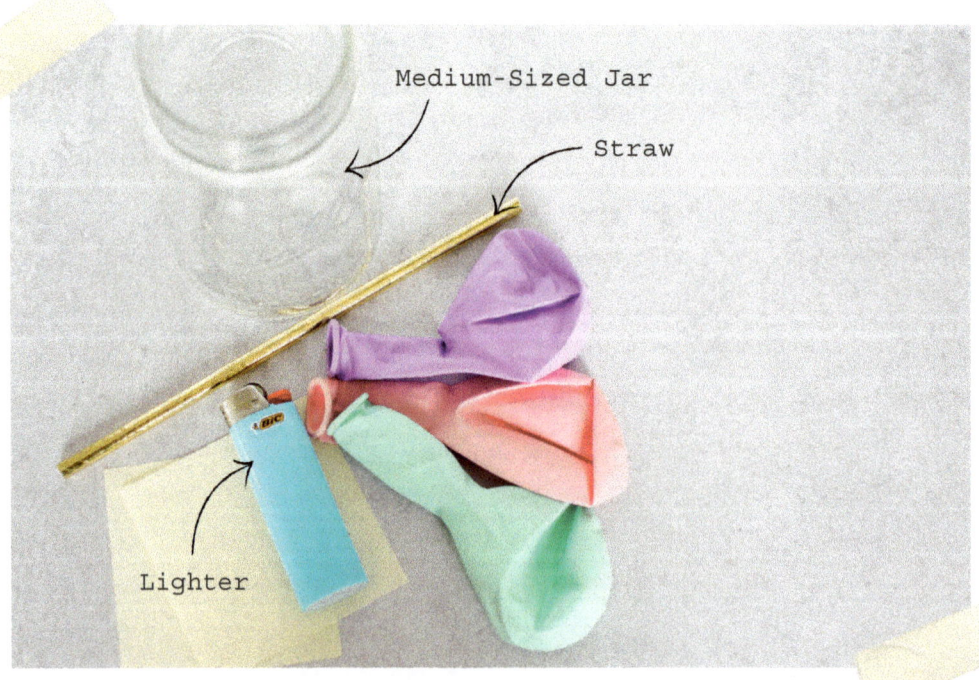

INSTRUCTIONS

1. Connect the balloon's opening to a faucet.
2. Put some water in the balloon so it is a bit bigger than the bottle's opening.

3. Tie a knot at the balloon's neck.
4. Make the bottle rim a bit wet, then have kids push the balloon into the bottle. Ask:

    "Can the balloon fit into the bottle?"
    (**Answer:** *No*)

5. Remove the balloon from the bottle and place it on the table.

6. Use a lighter or match to burn a small strip of paper (or folded post-it note).

7. Drop the burning strip of paper into the bottle.

8. Place the balloon on the bottle again. Observe how the balloon jiggles and starts getting pulled into the bottle slowly.

9. Once the balloon stops moving into the bottle, try to take the "stuck" balloon out of the bottle. Say:.

    "Can you remove the balloon?"

    "The balloon is stuck because no air could get around it."

10. Take a straw and put it between the stuck balloon and the bottle edge while pulling the balloon out. The balloon should come off the bottle easily. *Voila*!

Stuck Balloon

The straw releases the balloon from the jar

Discussion

1. What can we learn from our activity today?

   _____
   _____
   _____

   Think of the balloon as us. The fire and the pressure inside the bottle are like the *temptation* we face every day.

   At times, we might feel the need to do what others do so we can fit in or be liked. This is called "peer pressure." Peer pressure can pull us into temptations.

   (Note to parents: There will be more detailed talk about peer pressure in Bible Comes to Life: Book 4.)

2. Have you ever felt tempted? What are some things kids usually struggle with? Share real-life stories or examples when you feel tempted to do something wrong.
   (Parents can share their experiences too.)

   _____
   _____
   _____

3. How did the straw help the stuck balloon? Who acts like the straw in our daily life?

   _____
   _____
   _____

   (Answer: *The straw helps free the stuck balloon by letting air into the bottle. This evens out the air pressure inside and outside, so we can easily take the balloon out.)*

   The straw is like God in our life. He will always show us a way out when temptations pull us in.

   (Refer to the Fact Check section for the science behind this experiment.)

2-2 Temptations: "Just One Bite!"

4. Read **1 Corinthians 10:13** and share what you learn from this verse.

> "The temptations in your life are no different from what others experience. And **God is faithful.** He will not allow the temptation to be more than you can stand. When you are tempted, he will show you a **way out** so that you can endure."

5. Do you think it's wrong to be tempted? Is it wrong for the fish to want to eat the fat, juicy worm on the hook?

(**Answer:** *It's not wrong to be tempted. Even Jesus was tempted in Matthew 4:1–11. But, it is wrong to give in to those temptations and do things that lead us to sin.*)

When we are tempted, God will show us a way out. However, **it's our choice whether we accept His help or not. Sometimes, accepting His help might mean making choices that are not popular**. It could mean saying "no" to party invites, "no" to following the crowd, "no" to cheating, or "no" to that "one bite."

Summary

Remember, we should quickly **run from temptations**. One wrong choice can lead to a bigger problem. Sin can turn into a hard-to-break habit. It drags us in deeper, just like the stuck balloon.

We can also defeat temptations **using God's Word**, just as Jesus did. Use a truth from the Bible to counter the lies of the devil. This is our strongest weapon. For instance, say, "My body is the Holy Spirit's temple, so I'll honor God with it," when tempted to eat or drink something we shouldn't.

Get away from the bait, not toward it. Say no to "just one bite."

2-2 Temptations: "Just One Bite!"

Truth to Remember

In life, we will get tempted.

Don't take "just one bite," or we'll get hooked!

… God is faithful….
When you are tempted, he will show you
a way out so that you can endure.

1 Corinthians 10:13

FACT CHECK

WHAT IS SIN?

The word "sin" in the Bible can mean two things:[1]

- ☑ The first meaning is **"transgression"** (crossing limits or boundaries). In a soccer or basketball game, players must stay within the set area. Going outside the boundaries leads to a penalty.

  Sin means *going beyond the boundaries* God set for us.

- ☑ The second meaning of sin is **"missing the mark."** Think of a player aiming for a goal but missing. That player does not score.

  Sin is like *missing the goal:* God's perfect plan for us. Sin damages our relationship with our Creator.

Sin isn't just breaking God's laws (like lying or stealing). The Bible also says, "Remember, it is sin to know what you ought to do and then not do it" (James 4:17).

THE SCIENCE BEHIND "THE BALLOON VS. THE BOTTLE" EXPERIMENT

The balloon gets sucked into the bottle because of air pressure difference.

At first, the air pressure inside and outside the bottle is the same. When we put a burning paper inside, it heats the air in the bottle. The warm air expands and takes more space. It moves the balloon around while trying to escape from the bottle. You might see the balloon shaking as air rushes out.

After the fire goes out (due to lack of oxygen), the air in the bottle cools down and takes up less space. But as the balloon blocks the way out, new air can't enter. This makes a low-pressure area inside the bottle. The outside air pressure is greater, pushing part of the balloon into the bottle. Slowly, the balloon gets pulled inside the bottle.

2-3

The Invisible Enemy

2-3 The Invisible Enemy

PURPOSE

To show our children that we have an unseen enemy who always tries to steal, kill, and destroy our destinies in God.

To remind them that Jesus, on the contrary, came to give us an abundant life.

Icebreaker

- Is there someone at school or home you see as an "enemy" or someone who annoys you?
- What do you do when you have to meet or talk to them?

2-3 The Invisible Enemy

The world has all kinds of people. People have different habits, personalities, and opinions. For instance, if you like things tidy but have friends who are noisy and have messy desks, it might bother you. How would you feel working with such friends? It could be frustrating, right?

. . .

NON-BIBLICAL VIEW

As we discussed before, certain people can easily upset us or make us angry. We might even consider them as **enemies**: people we want to stay away from or fight against.

Have you heard of the phrase: "Birds of a feather flock together"? It means people with similar personalities and interests tend to stick together. It's easier to be friends with those who are like us. People who differ might seem like opponents or enemies.

But are they truly our real enemy?

2-3 The Invisible Enemy

BIBLICAL VIEW

The truth is they are *not* our real enemies. God intentionally places them in our lives to help us grow to be a better person. **Proverbs 27:17** says, "As iron sharpens iron, so a friend sharpens a friend."

Maybe God puts them around us to teach us **patience**. Being around them allows us to be more graceful towards people who are different from us. We can also learn to show **kindness** and *serve* these people, instead of being annoyed by them. Or maybe, God brings them to us so we can **join forces against the real enemy**.

So, who is our real enemy?
What does the enemy want from us?

Check out what the Bible says in **1 Peter 5:8**:

Stay alert! Watch out for your great enemy, the devil. He prowls around like a roaring lion, looking for someone to devour.

Our main enemy is the devil! Jesus warned us that the enemy's goal is **"to steal, kill, and destroy"** (John 10:10). But we don't need to be scared because Jesus defeated this enemy when He died on the cross.

The devil is the unseen enemy who tries to steal our peace, kill our joy, and destroy our purpose in God.

Today, we will play a game to learn about our invisible enemy.

2-3 The Invisible Enemy

Activity

Eagle Vs. Chicken Game

MATERIALS

Optional: a blanket or any silly props for the "Enemy"

Note: *This game needs at least three people. Make sure the room is safe for running around.*

INSTRUCTIONS

1. Introduce the "Eagle and Chicken" game.

   *"Have you heard of the **'Eagle and Chicken'** game? Kids play it in China, Greece, Turkey, and other places. If it's new to you, here's a quick explanation.*

   *In this game, players act like an **eagle** (the enemy), a **mother hen**, or **chicks**. At the beginning, the chicks stand behind the mother hen in a line. The first chick holds onto the hen's waist or clothes. The next chick holds onto the first, and so on. The hen tries to shield her chicks from the eagle by stretching her arms at shoulder height.*

   Once the game begins, the eagle can run anywhere to catch the chicks. If the eagle catches a chick, that chick follows the eagle. The eagle keeps trying to catch the other chicks..

   Meanwhile, the mother hen aims to rescue the chicks caught by the eagle and protect the rest."

2-3 The Invisible Enemy

2. In our game today, we are adding a small twist to the names:
   - The eagle becomes the "Enemy."
   - The mother hen turns into the "Protector."
   - The chicks are now the "Followers."

3. The goal of the Enemy is to catch the children and make them his/her followers by tagging them. **Important:** No pulling or rough play is allowed.

   Tips:
   - *Choose Dad (or the tallest person in the family) to be the Enemy.*
   - *The Enemy can wear a cape or blanket and act silly. (Not scary! We want it fun, not frightening. Think of a "tickle monster" vibe when chasing the kids.) It's a great chance for Dad to be goofy and for everyone to enjoy family time together.*

4. Choose someone else (Mom or an older child) to be the "Protector." The Protector's role is to shield the children behind them and rescue the caught children from the Enemy by tagging them.

5. Make sure everyone gets ready: The Enemy faces the Protector, and the other children stand in line behind the Protector. The Followers should hold onto the waist or clothing of the person in front of them.

6. Explain the game rules:

   "Remember, stick close to your Protector no matter what. Hold onto the Protector and to each other really tight. Don't let the Enemy trick you or split you up! If the Enemy tags you, go to the back of the Enemy's line. But don't worry, your Protector will try to save you from the Enemy."

   Note: *The Enemy's job is to* **distract**, **divide**, *and* **deceive** *the kids (like saying, 'Hey, who's at the door?' or 'Look, big squirrels outside!'). When the kids get distracted, tag them.*

7. Have fun and play as much as you like!

Discussion

1. How did you feel when the Enemy started chasing you?

2. Who was the person the Enemy could easily distract? What do you think will happen if the team members argue and get separated? Will it be harder or easier for the Enemy to catch you?

3. What did you have to do to stay safe in the game?

This game teaches us how the devil works. He tries to **distract**, **divide**, and **deceive** us so he can ruin God's plans for us. When we're not paying attention, thinking about other things, and far from our Protector (Jesus), he can easily trap us. It's even easier for him if we're fighting or separated from each other.

Guess what? The people who annoy us or seem like enemies are actually our **teammates**. God wants us to stay together and be united, even if we're different. In **Matthew 12:25** (NIV), Jesus said, "Every kingdom divided against itself will be ruined, and every city or household divided against itself will not stand."

2-3 The Invisible Enemy

4. Can you think of things that might **divide** our family?

   _____
   _____
   _____

   (***Answer:** Some examples are fights, selfishness, and jealousy.)*

5. What are the things that can **distract** us from God's Word and what He wants us to do?

   _____
   _____
   _____

   (***Answer:** Some examples are too much screen time, too busy playing or working.)*

6. Lastly, can you share some **deceitful (false) things** you might come across at school, in the things you watch or read, or from your friends?

   _____
   _____
   _____

   (***Answer:** For example, "Your brothers and sisters, or even those friends who annoy you, are like enemies. Stay away from them."; "Your parents will never understand you"; "You're better on your own. You don't need family and friends to look out for you.")*

Summary

Even now, the enemy still tries to distract, divide, and deceive us from following God's perfect plan. His goal is to steal, kill, and destroy our destinies so we can't do the things God has planned for us.

But here's the good news: if we **stick close to Jesus** and **stay united with other believers**, the enemy can't win. Jesus came to give us a full and joyful life.

Truth to Remember

Annoying classmates or siblings are not our real enemies.

The devil is.

Stay close to Jesus and be united with each other.

For we are not fighting against
flesh-and-blood enemies,
but against evil rulers and authorities
of the unseen world.

Ephesians 6:12

NOTE: In the next lesson, you will cook and enjoy a meal together. You can start the lesson and the cooking activity right before your usual mealtime. Then, enjoy the meal while discussing the questions.

2-3 The Invisible Enemy

2-4

Unbreakable

2-4 Unbreakable

NOTE: The activity includes cooking and having a meal together. Plan and decide when you will begin the lesson in advance.

PURPOSE

To teach children that when they stay united, they become strong and cannot be broken by the enemy.

Icebreaker

- When you look at our friends and neighbors, which family do you think has the most fun together and enjoys being with each other the most? Why do you think so?

- Which family doesn't seem as close or spend much time together? Why do you think that?

- What do siblings or families usually argue about?

Last time, we talked about how the devil tries to divide our family. How does he do that? He makes us argue, causes fights between siblings, keeps parents busy, and many more. The enemy tries to make our hearts distant from each other.

In 1858, Abraham Lincoln made a speech and quoted Jesus' famous teaching in the Bible. He said, "**A house divided against itself cannot stand.**" What do you think this means?

. . .

NON-BIBLICAL VIEW

The world teaches us it's *totally normal* for siblings to fight. Many homes are filled with constant arguing. Parents' love grows cold. Families are busy with too many activities outside. Achievements, awards, and sports become more important, while staying together as a family becomes less important. So, many families end up divided.

BIBLICAL VIEW

The Bible, however, teaches that God wants His people to live in unity. King David wrote a song about it in **Psalm 133:1–3** (MSG):

> How wonderful, how beautiful,
> when brothers and sisters get along!…
> Yes, that's where GOD commands the blessing,
> ordains eternal life.

When we are united in our hearts, we become strong and unbreakable! **Ecclesiastes 4:12** (MSG) says:

> By yourself you're unprotected.
> With a friend you can face the worst.
> Can you round up a third?
> A three-stranded rope isn't easily snapped.

2-4 Unbreakable

What does it mean?

When we stay strong and united as a family, the enemy can't easily harm us.

Today, we will have so much fun as a family. We'll cook and enjoy a simple yet wonderful dish together.

2-4 Unbreakable

Activity

Rainbow Spaghetti

MATERIALS

- A large cooking pot
- One pound of uncooked spaghetti
- Four to six tablespoons melted butter (or olive oil)
- Food coloring (various colors)
- Sealable plastic sandwich bags (As many as the number of colors used. Use at least one color per person in the family.)
- Colander (to drain pasta)
- Freshly grated parmesan cheese (1 cup)
- Salt and pepper
- Water

Note: This modified buttered noodles recipe makes around 8 servings.

You can change the quantities based on your family size and preferences.

If you like, you can add other seasonings (e.g. garlic powder), garnish with chopped fresh Italian parsley, or add some proteins.

INSTRUCTIONS

1. Bring 4–6 quarts of water in a pot to a rolling boil. Add a pinch of salt to the water.

2. While waiting for the water to boil, take a single strand of spaghetti and show it to the kids. Say:

   "Just like this strand of spaghetti, the Bible tells us that when we're alone, we're vulnerable and can be easily broken."

   Snap the strand of spaghetti and invite the children to try snapping one too.

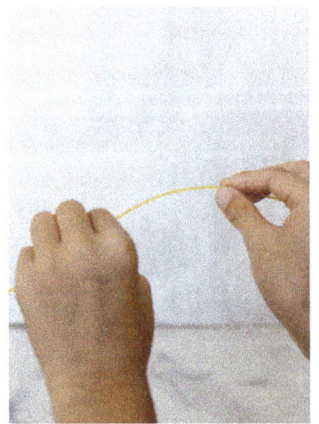 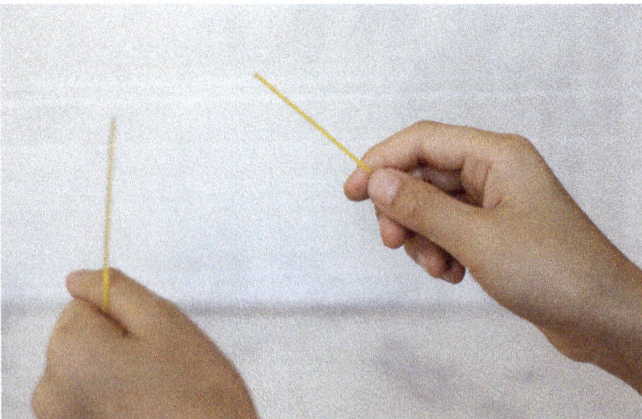

3. Hold a whole bundle of spaghetti together and try to break it in half. Take turns trying to snap the bundled spaghetti. As you do this, say:

   > *"See, it's hard to break the spaghetti when it's in a bundle. Likewise, alone we are weak, but when we stay united as a family and community, we are strong!"*

   > *"Now, let's cook the spaghetti. We will see how beautiful and wonderful it is for brothers and sisters to live in unity."*

4. Put the spaghetti into the boiling water and cook over medium heat until tender yet firm to the bite. Follow the package instructions for cooking time.
5. While the spaghetti is cooking, add two tablespoons of water and a few drops of food coloring to each sandwich bag. Use a different color for each bag.
6. Check if the spaghetti is cooked by tasting it (be careful, it's hot!)
7. Drain the cooked spaghetti.
8. Divide the cooked spaghetti into the bags with different food colors.

9. Seal the sandwich bags and shake them to coat the spaghetti with colors.
10. Take out the colored spaghetti from the bags and rinse it with cold water to remove extra coloring.

11. Mix the different colored spaghetti in a big bowl with melted butter (or olive oil).

12. Season with salt and pepper.

13. Sprinkle parmesan cheese on top and mix it all together.

14. Serve and enjoy the rainbow spaghetti as a family! You can also have a discussion while eating.

Discussion

1. What do you think of our rainbow spaghetti?

   _____
   _____
   _____
   _____

   Each color in the spaghetti is like one of us in this family. We each have our own distinct "color" and personality. However, can you see how beautiful and fun it is when brothers and sisters live together in unity?

2. Let's talk about each family member's strengths and weaknesses. For example, what do you think big brother is good at? What are some things he might find challenging? Take turns to share your thoughts and ideas.

   _____
   _____
   _____
   _____

3. Each of us has our unique way of thinking, feeling, and acting, which is our personality. We also have different habits. Can you notice any differences between the personalities and habits of A and B (*mention two family members' names*)?

   _____
   _____
   _____
   _____

4. Some of these differences might bother or annoy us. But the Bible teaches us to love each other just as we love ourselves (Matthew 22:39).

How can we practice accepting each other's differences and living in unity? (Read **1 Peter 3:8-9** MSG for some ideas.)

> Summing up: Be **agreeable,** be **sympathetic,** be **loving,** be **compassionate,** be **humble.**
> That goes for all of you, no exceptions.
> No retaliation [meaning don't repay evil for evil].
> No sharp-tongued sarcasm.
> Instead, **bless**—that's your job, to bless.
> You'll be a blessing and also get a blessing.

5. Besides your family, who do you see as your *main community*? (These are the people you spend time with and feel close to, like "brothers and sisters" in Christ.)

6. Which do you prefer: living like a single strand of spaghetti all alone and divided, or living in unity with your family and community, so you can be strong and unbreakable against the enemy?

Summary

We are all special with unique gifts and talents from God.
Never compare yourself to others. **Embrace** differences. Live in **peace and unity**.

Alone we are weak, but together with our family and community, we are strong.

2-4 Unbreakable

Truth to Remember

Alone we are weak. But together, we are strong.

By yourself, you are unprotected.
With a friend you can face the worst...
A three-stranded rope isn't easily
snapped.

Ecclesiastes 4:12 (MSG)

FACT CHECK

SIBLING RIVALRY IN THE BIBLE

The first story of murder in the Bible involves two brothers: **Cain** and **Abel** (Genesis 4:1-16). What do you think made Cain kill Abel?

The Bible tells us it began when Cain **compared** himself to his brother, got really angry, and lost control. God warned him that if he doesn't control his anger, sin is ready to take over him (v. 7).

This story teaches us that jealousy and anger can lead to harmful actions.

Have you ever been very angry at your siblings or parents? If so, how do you think you should handle your anger?

. . .

The stories of **Jacob** and **Esau,** as well as **Joseph** and his **brothers** also show sibling rivalry. All these stories start with **jealousy and comparing** themselves to others.

Remember, "comparison is the thief of joy." Instead of comparing, let's practice being thankful for what we have and always give our best effort to live in unity.

2-5

A Fallen World

2-5 A Fallen World

PURPOSE

To understand that God gives us free will to choose.
To understand that we live in a broken and fallen world because of sin.

Icebreaker

- If you could have any animal as a pet, which one would you choose and why?
- Which one would you prefer: having a real pet or a robot pet?

Have you noticed lately any unfair things happening at school or in your neighborhood? There are many bad things happening in the world today, like the global pandemic, war, sickness, death, natural disasters, racism, and many more.

You might start to wonder, "Why did this happen?" Or, if you are the one facing these challenges, you might ask, "Why is this happening to me?" "Why is my family going through this?"

. . .

NON-BIBLICAL VIEW

If you have wondered about these questions, you're not alone. Many others have asked similar things. Here are some common questions:

> Where is God when bad things happen?
>
> Why didn't He prevent disasters?
>
> Is God punishing me for something my family or I did?
>
> If God is good and powerful, why does He allow bad things?
>
> Why doesn't God punish the bad people instead?

Some people believe the bad things in the world prove there is no God. (These people are called "atheists.")

BIBLICAL VIEW

The Bible can provide answers to these tough questions. When God made humans, He gave us the freedom to make choices, which is called **free will**. This means that we can choose to do good or bad things, to obey or disobey God.

God loves us, but He doesn't force us to love Him back. Imagine if we're like robots, only saying "I love you" when God pushes a button. Those words would not be meaningful because they do not come from our hearts. It is not genuine love.

God gives us free will to choose. He wants us to love and obey Him because we *want* to, not because we *have* to.

It's similar to how we enjoy having real pets rather than robot pets. Real pets gives us true friendship and love, not something forced or fake.

But when people are free to choose, there is a big chance of humans choosing sin over God and failing to obey Him. Did God know this might happen before He made the first humans? Absolutely! Still, God took that **huge risk** anyway because He wanted **a special and real relationship** with humans.

True enough, in the midst of God's beautiful garden of Eden, Adam and Eve fell into sin. As a result of this, God told Adam, "Since you listened to your wife and ate from the tree whose fruit I commanded you not to eat, **the ground is cursed** because of you…" (Genesis 3:17).

A cursed ground means natural disasters, diseases, and war. The **whole creation now suffers** because of it (Romans 8:22). It was not God's idea for humans to live in a broken world. It was human sin that led us here.

Because of humans' disobedience, we now live in a "fallen world."

Let's do an activity to remember these ideas. We'll create something special!

2-5 A Fallen World

Scratch Art

MATERIALS

- White paper (Thicker materials will work better.)
- Wax crayons or oil pastels
- Black crayon or acrylic paint
- Toothpick (or other pointy objects, such as skewers, chopsticks, screwdriver, or paperclip)
- Paintbrush (optional—if using black acrylic paint)
- Picture frames (optional—to display the art creations)

Note: Guide the activity step by step without revealing the next steps or the final goal. You can also cut the paper into a smaller size, like 4 x 6 inches, to make it easier to work with and fit into a small picture frame.

2-5 A Fallen World

INSTRUCTIONS

1. Use crayons or oil pastels to make abstract art on a white paper. Fill the paper with colorful patterns or shapes until it's all covered, making it as beautiful and colorful as possible.

   Note: Do not use black color in this step.

2. **Optional:** For an extra twist, exchange pictures with each other and let family members color the pictures black in the next step. This can create a surprise reaction, but avoid this step if it upsets the children too much to see their creations being "ruined" by others.

3. Completely cover the colorful patterns with black crayon or acrylic paint. If you're using paint, make sure to wait until it dries before moving on to the next step.

4. **Optional:** If you swapped pictures earlier, return them to their owners.

5. Once the black paint is dry, it's time for scratch art. Use a toothpick or something pointy to draw pictures, write messages, or even make a family portrait. If you make a mistake, cover it with black crayon or paint, and wait for it to dry before scratching again.

2-5 A Fallen World

1. Share your artwork with your family and explain your piece. What do you like about each other's creations?

   _____
   _____
   _____
   _____

2. How did you feel when you were asked to color your colorful patterns all black? Were you surprised by the request?

   _____
   _____
   _____
   _____

   Do you remember what God said when He finished creating everything? He said it was *very good*! Like the beautiful patterns you made earlier in your art, God initially created a perfect world without sin.

   But then, humans decided to disobey God. Adam and Eve ate the forbidden fruit, and sin entered the world. Like your whole artwork turned dark, the fallen world became broken and cursed because of sin. Diseases, suffering, and natural disasters are all results of sin.

3. What tools did you use to create the beautiful art on the black picture? How did these tools help in our activity?

   _____
   _____
   _____
   _____

   (**Answer:** *We used sharp tools to remove the black paint/crayon and reveal the colorful patterns underneath.*)

2-5 A Fallen World

Just like how we used sharp tools earlier, God can also use our tough times to remind us of our purpose and draw us closer to Him. Sometimes, even challenging things like sickness, suffering, or problems can help us see things differently and bring us closer to God. .

(You can read about "Jesus and a blind man" in the Fact Check section for more on this.)

4. When you turned the black picture into something good, it shows us that God can bring good out of the bad things that happen to us. This reminds us of Joseph's story in the Bible. Do you remember what happened to him?

_____

_____

_____

Joseph's brothers planned to harm him and sold him as a slave, but God turned this bad situation into something good to later save the Israelites. In **Genesis 50:20**, Joseph said to his brothers:

> "You intended to harm me, but God **intended it all for good.** He brought me to this position so I could save the lives of many people."

5. Have you ever had something good out of a bad situation? Share an example of the good things that came from a tough moment.

_____

_____

_____

Suppose you experienced the COVID-19 pandemic where everyone had to stay home for a long time. What good things did you learn during this challenging time? For example, more family time, a chance to help others, no need to set a morning alarm (school in pajamas!), etc.

6. Read God's promise to us in **Romans 8:28** (NIV).

> And we know that in all things **God works for the good** of those who love him, who have been called according to his purpose.

God also has a plan to make everything perfect again. One day, He will take us away from all the bad things (Romans 8:21).

Summary

God did not create evil; He gave us the power to choose. When people choose to disobey, we end up in a broken world because of sin.

Thankfully, God sent **His Son to save us** from our sins. He also gives us the **Holy Spirit** to be our **special helper**. Even though life can be tough because of sin, we have a **mighty God** who can turn bad situations into good. He sees more than we do and has the power to make things better.

Truth to Remember

We live in a fallen world because of human sin.

And we know that in all things God works for the good of those who love him…

Romans 8:28 (NIV)

2-5 A Fallen World

FACT CHECK

HAVE YOU HEARD THE STORY OF JESUS AND A BLIND MAN?

Read the story in John 9:1-11.

Is the blindness a punishment for something bad that he did? Or is it because of his parents?

Jesus said, "This happened so the power of God could be seen in him" (v. 3). The blind man got to tell others about the miracle he experienced (v. 10-11).

2-5 A Fallen World

2-6
A Clean Heart

2-6 A Clean Heart

PURPOSE

To learn about humans' sinful nature. To teach our children to run to God and not away from Him when they sin.

Icebreaker

- Have you ever done something wrong and felt scared or embarrassed to admit it?
- Which is more challenging: pointing out others' mistakes or admitting our own?

Before, we discussed how sin came into the world. Since then, as **Romans 3:23** says, we all fall short of God's perfect standard. Even if we try our best to follow God's commands, we can't do it perfectly by ourselves.

No one is flawless, and we all make mistakes. Let's be honest. What do we usually do when we mess up? Do we admit it right away, or do we try to hide it? Do we blame others or come up with excuses?

<blockquote>
"It wasn't me."
"He did it first!"
"They forced me to do it."
"She started it!"
</blockquote>

Do these sound familiar to you?

When God spoke to Adam about his mistake, he didn't admit his fault. Instead, he blamed Eve, who in turn blamed the snake. Just like them, admitting our mistakes right away isn't our first reaction when we mess up. It's a tough thing to do!

• • •

NON-BIBLICAL VIEW

People often hide their mistakes. When caught, they might make excuses for their actions.

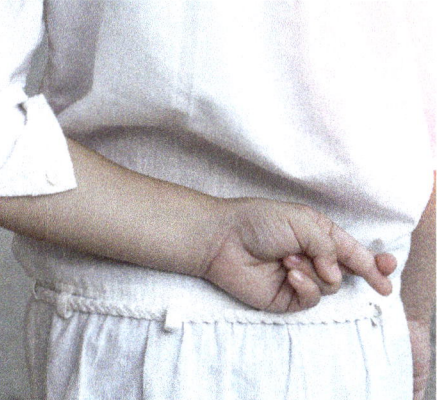

The world might say it's fine to hide our mistakes and keep quiet about them, especially if no one knows. And if we get caught, try to find good excuses to defend ourselves, lie about it, or shift the blame to others. Just do anything so we don't look bad or get into trouble.

BIBLICAL VIEW

Let's see what the Bible says about this. Do you remember what Adam and Eve did after they ate the forbidden fruit? Yes, they hid from God! Here's what happened in **Genesis 3:8–9**:

> When the cool evening breezes were blowing, the man and his wife heard the LORD God walking about in the garden. So they hid from the LORD God among the trees. Then the LORD God called to the man, "Where are you?"

Did God really not know where Adam and Eve were? Of course He knew! He knows everything. When He called out to them, He was giving them a **chance to come clean** before Him. But instead of being honest, Adam and Eve started blaming each other. "She gave it to me!" "No, the snake made me do it."

Imagine finding a rotten fish in your home by accident. You wouldn't want to hide it under your bed, right? The bad smell would spread, germs would come, and soon the whole house will smell like garbage. *Yikes!*

> Likewise, when we sin, we can't just hide it and pretend it didn't happen.

Instead, we should run to God and ask for forgiveness. We also need to admit our mistakes and say sorry to those we've wronged.

Today, we'll learn that admitting our mistakes is better than hiding them. God is always ready to forgive us, and only He can wipe away our sins (Isaiah 43:25).

2-6 A Clean Heart

Activity

Sin Jars

MATERIALS
- Clear jars or drinking glasses—one for each family member
- Food coloring
- Condiments, such as soy sauce, fish sauce, tomato ketchup, or vinegar (optional)
- Water

Clear Jars

Fish Sauce (for dramatic effect)

Condiments

2-6 A Clean Heart

INSTRUCTIONS

1. Give a jar to each family member.
2. Fill the jars with clean water.
3. Gather and sit around a table.
4. Ask family members to put the jars in front of them. Say:

   "These jars are like our hearts. God created us with clean hearts. However, because sin entered the world, we can't avoid making mistakes."

   "Romans 3:23 says everybody sins, and we all fall short of the glory of God."

5. Take turns sharing examples of past mistakes or sins—whether you did it on purpose or it was an accident, big or small, serious or silly, caught or not caught.

   As each person shares, add a drop of food coloring to their jar. For instance, someone might say, "I lied to my mom when I was five," and you'll add a drop of red food coloring to their jar.

   Note: Start with a parent sharing first. This way, kids see that parents are also imperfect. It's a chance for parents to show vulnerability and humility, creating an environment where kids feel safe sharing their own mistakes in the future.

6. Continue taking turns sharing past mistakes. Feel free to go around as many times as you'd like.

   To make it more impactful, add condiments or spices to the jars as you go, creating a stronger smell and showing that we can't hide the unpleasant effects of sin.

7. Once everyone has their jar filled with the colored water, take the jars to the sink.

2-6 A Clean Heart

8. One by one, place the "dirty" jars under the faucet and turn on the water. As the dirty water gets washed away and replaced by clean water, say:

   "The water from the faucet represents God's love, always ready to pour into our sinful hearts."

   "When we come to God and admit our mistakes, He will not be angry. Instead, He loves and welcomes us."

   "Like the clean water replaces the dirty water, His endless love will fill us up, making our hearts clean once more. He loves us no matter what."

1. What did you learn from today's activity?

God said, "Though your sins are like **scarlet**, I will make them as white as snow. Though they are red like **crimson**, I will make them as white as wool" (Isaiah 1:18).

Crimson and scarlet are intense and bright red colors. It's amazing that God can make us clean and pure like snow again!

2. Did you quickly confess the mistakes we talked about earlier? What's the most serious consequence you've faced from your mistake?

3. Why do you think people hide their mistakes or sins?

(**Answer:** *too embarrassed, afraid of punishment, ignorant, feeling self-righteous*)

4. What will happen if you keep the dirty and smelly jar under your bed instead of being honest and cleaning it under the faucet?

_____
_____
_____
_____

(**Answer:** *It could spill and create a bigger mess. The bad smell might get worse and spread throughout the whole house.*)

5. What will happen if you keep hiding your sins or mistakes instead of running to God or telling your parents?

_____
_____
_____
_____

(**Answer:** *If you continue hiding your sins or mistakes, the situation might get worse. It's like leaving the dirty jar under the bed–the problem could become bigger and more difficult to handle.* **Numbers 32:23** *says, "Your sin will find you out." We can't hide our sins forever.*)

6. Read **Psalm 103:8–13** (NIrV). Each family member can take turns reading.

> The LORD is **tender** and **kind**. He is **gracious**.
> He is **slow to get angry**. He is **full of love**.
> He won't keep bringing charges against us.
> He won't stay angry with us forever.
> He doesn't punish us for our sins as much as we should be punished.
> He doesn't pay us back in keeping with the evil things we've done.

> He loves those who have respect for him.
> His love is as high as the heavens are above the earth.
> He has removed our sins from us.
> … as far as the east is from the west.
> A father is tender and kind to his children.
> In the same way, the LORD is **tender** and **kind**
> to those who have respect for him.

What can we learn about God from these verses?

_____

_____

_____

Admitting our mistakes doesn't mean we can avoid the consequences or punishment. Adam and Eve faced consequences for their actions too.

However, even after God disciplined them, He showed **mercy**. God made clothes from animal skins to cover them (Genesis 3:21). God forgives us and shows His mercy as well.

Summary

When we make mistakes, let's **turn to Jesus, not away** from Him. Confess your sins to Him. He will give mercy and forgiveness to wash away your sins.

Hiding sins will make things worse. Don't hide the "dirty jar" or "rotten fish" under your bed! Run to God instead, and let Him give you a clean heart.

Truth to Remember

When we make mistakes, run to Jesus, not away from Him.

But if we confess our sins to him,
he is faithful and just to forgive us our sins
and to cleanse us from all wickedness.

1 John 1:9

2-6 A Clean Heart

Truth Blast!

. . .

Here's a list of all Truths to Remember and the memory verses from this book for a quick reference and reminders. The powerful Truths in these pages will help your family stand up against the enemy's lies. The Bible says to "repeat them again and again." Talk about them when you are at home, on the road, going to bed, and getting up (See Deuteronomy 6:7). You may create a memory card for each Truth and Bible verse, ask children to write the Truths in their journals, or have a quick quiz during car rides.

1

God alone is the source of truth.
God's Word in the Bible tells us the real truth.

> *Study this Book of Instruction continually.*
> *Meditate on it day and night*
> *so you will be sure to obey everything written in it.*
> *Only then will you prosper and succeed in all you do.*
>
> — *Joshua 1:8*

2

In life, we will get tempted.
Don't take "just one bite," or we'll get hooked!

> *… God is faithful….*
> *When you are tempted, he will show you a way out*
> *so that you can endure.*
>
> — *1 Corinthians 10:13*

3. Annoying classmates or siblings are not our real enemies. The devil is. Stay close to Jesus and be united with each other.

> *For we are not fighting against flesh-and-blood enemies,*
> *but against evil rulers and authorities of the unseen world.*
> — *Ephesians 6:12*

4. Alone we are weak.
But together, we are strong.

> *By yourself, you are unprotected.*
> *With a friend you can face the worst…*
> *A three-stranded rope isn't easily snapped.*
> — *Ecclesiastes 4:12 (MSG)*

5. We live in a fallen world because of human sin.

> *And we know that in all things*
> *God works for the good of those who love him…*
> — *Romans 8:28 (NIV)*

 When we make mistakes, run to Jesus, not away from Him.

But if we confess our sins to him, he is faithful and just to forgive us our sins and to cleanse us from all wickedness.

— 1 John 1:9

For family:

Jesus is the absolute Truth. He alone is "the way, the truth, and the life" (John 14:6). As a family, commit to using God's Word as the true guide and standard. Remind each other who the real enemy is and stand together despite mistakes, failures, and disappointment.

For parents:

The world may seem out of control. We can't avoid curses, pain, suffering, fights, and death. Parents, God is still in control. May the words in Psalm 55:22 be an encouragement for you today as you raise your children: "Give your burdens to the LORD, and he will take care of you. He will not permit the godly to slip and fall." God's got this!

Notes

Unless otherwise noted, all websites were last accessed on 1/6/2021.

2-1: True or False?

1. "Bible Facts for Kids," Biblical-Literacy, biblical-literacy.weebly.com/bible-facts-for-kids.html.
2. Cedric Van den Berg, "Curious Kids: How Does an Optical Illusion Work?" The Conversation, October 23, 2019, theconversation.com/curious-kids-how-does-an-optical-illusion-work-123008.
3. Ken Boa, "How Accurate Is the Bible?" Reflections Ministries, kenboa.org/apologetics/how-accurate-is-the-bible/.
4. Sid Litke, "Is the Bible Reliable?—Seven Questions," Bible.org, January 6, 2012, bible.org/article/bible-reliable%E2%80%94seven-questions.

2-2: Temptations: "Just One Bite!"

1. Scott Ashley, "How Does the Bible Define Sin?" Beyond Today, United Church of God, March 29, 1997, https://www.ucg.org/the-good-news/how-does-the-bible-define-sin.

2-1: True or False?
Rahul Pandit / Pexels
Pictrider / Shutterstock.com
Sixteen Miles Out / Unsplash
Fwstudio / Freepik.com
SkazovD / Shutterstock.com
Pisannoah / Shutterstock.com
Standret / Freepik

2-2: Temptations: "Just One Bite!"
Markus Spiske / Unsplash
Alexandr Podvalny / Pexels
Will Walker / Unsplash
zenad nabil / Unsplash
Mael Balland / Unsplash

2-3: The Invisible Enemy
Lisa H / Unsplash
Ferenc Horvath / Unsplash
RODNAE Productions / Pexels
30000011348 / Lovepik.com
Jcomp / Freepik.com

2-4: Unbreakable
Glen Carrie / Unsplash
fizkes / Shutterstock.com
Liderina / Shutterstock.com
Graystudiopro1 / Freepik.com

2-5: A Fallen World
алесь-усцінаў / Pexels
Alvan Nee / Shutterstock.com
Xolodan / Shutterstock.com
Kelly / Pexels
Pixabay / Pexels
Sviatoslav_Shevchenko / Shutterstock.com

2-6: A Clean Heart
Rahul Pandit / Pexels
Gpointstudio / Freepik.com
KayaMe / Shutterstock.com
BlurryMe / Shutterstock.com
Tatiana Syrikova / Pexels

Truth Blast!
Admiral General M. Godshepherdly / Pexels

Pages 4-7 and all Activities
Joy Sukadi

About the Authors

Joy Sukadi is a wife, mom of three, and a passionate preacher of God's Word. She has mentored and taught Jesus to women in her community in the past twenty years. She is currently pursuing a Theology Degree at Portland Bible School. Joy also runs a photography business and sees this as an opportunity to connect with local moms. In her spare time, she loves to bike with her family, hike the beautiful Pacific Northwest, do arts and crafts, and play games with her kids. She can't live without Jesus, coffee, and a series of good books.

Lilyana Margaretha is a wife and mom of two girls. She is passionate about equipping Christian parents on how to raise their kids with a biblical worldview. She has a doctoral degree in Molecular and Cellular Biology from the University of Washington. She has a vision of connecting science and the Bible, making it logical, relevant, and applicable in children's lives. Lilyana loves to make crafts, do science with her kids, and enjoy the beauty of the Pacific Northwest with her family.